TRADIT
INDONESIAN
COOKBOOK

AVA BAKER

CONTENTS

APPETIZERS

Satay Ayam (Chicken Satay)

Servings: 4 Time: 1 hour

Ingredients:

- *500g chicken breast, cut into cubes*
- *2 tablespoons soy sauce*
- *1 tablespoon honey*
- *1 teaspoon ground coriander*

- *1 teaspoon ground cumin*
- *1 teaspoon turmeric powder*
- *2 cloves garlic, minced*
- *1 shallot, finely chopped*
- *Bamboo skewers, soaked in water*

Directions:

1. *In a bowl, mix soy sauce, honey, ground coriander, ground cumin, turmeric powder, minced garlic, and chopped shallot to make the marinade.*
2. *Add the chicken cubes to the marinade, ensuring they are well coated. Marinate for at least 30 minutes.*
3. *Thread the marinated chicken onto bamboo skewers.*
4. *Preheat a grill or grill pan over medium-high heat.*
5. *Grill the chicken skewers for about 8-10 minutes, turning occasionally, until cooked through and slightly charred.*
6. *Serve hot with peanut sauce and cucumber slices on the side.*

Lumpia Semarang (Semarang Spring Rolls)

Servings: 4 Time: 45 minutes

Ingredients:

- *200g ground chicken or pork*
- *1 cup shredded cabbage*
- *1 carrot, julienned*
- *1 onion, finely chopped*
- *2 cloves garlic, minced*
- *1 tablespoon soy sauce*
- *1 tablespoon oyster sauce*
- *1 teaspoon sugar*
- *Salt and pepper to taste*
- *Lumpia wrappers (spring roll wrappers)*
- *Cooking oil for frying*

Directions:

1. *In a pan, heat some oil over medium heat. Add minced garlic and chopped onion, and sauté until fragrant.*
2. *Add ground chicken or pork to the pan and cook until browned.*

3. *Stir in shredded cabbage, julienned carrot, soy sauce, oyster sauce, sugar, salt, and pepper. Cook for a few minutes until the vegetables are tender.*

4. *Remove the mixture from heat and let it cool slightly.*

5. *Place a spoonful of the filling onto a lumpia wrapper and roll it tightly, folding the sides in as you roll.*

6. *Seal the edge of the wrapper with a bit of water to secure the roll.*

7. *Heat oil in a deep frying pan or pot over medium-high heat.*

8. *Fry the spring rolls until golden brown and crispy, turning occasionally to ensure even cooking.*

9. *Remove from oil and drain on paper towels.*

10. *Serve hot with sweet chili sauce or dipping sauce of your choice.*

Soto Ayam (Indonesian Chicken Soup)

Servings: 4 Time: 1 hour

Ingredients:

- *500g chicken pieces (bone-in for flavor)*
- *1 liter water*
- *2 stalks lemongrass, bruised*
- *3 kaffir lime leaves*
- *2 bay leaves*
- *3 cloves garlic, minced*
- *1 onion, finely chopped*
- *1 teaspoon ground turmeric*
- *Salt and pepper to taste*
- *200g vermicelli noodles, cooked according to package instructions*
- *2 boiled eggs, halved*
- *Fried shallots for garnish*
- *Chopped green onions for garnish*
- *Lime wedges for serving*
- *Sambal (optional, for extra spice)*

Directions:

1. In a pot, combine chicken pieces, water, lemongrass, kaffir lime leaves, bay leaves, minced garlic, chopped onion, ground turmeric, salt, and pepper.

2. Bring the soup to a boil, then reduce heat and let it simmer for about 30-40 minutes until the chicken is tender and cooked through.

3. Remove the chicken pieces from the soup and shred the meat. Set aside.

4. Strain the soup to remove the lemongrass, kaffir lime leaves, bay leaves, and any impurities, leaving a clear broth.

5. To serve, place some cooked vermicelli noodles in a bowl. Add shredded chicken and a boiled egg half.

6. Ladle the hot broth over the noodles and chicken.

7. Garnish with fried shallots, chopped green onions, and a lime wedge.

8. Serve hot with sambal on the side for those who prefer extra spice.

Martabak Manis (Sweet Pancake)

Servings: 4 Time: 45 minutes

Ingredients:

- *1 cup all-purpose flour*
- *1/2 cup granulated sugar*
- *1 teaspoon baking powder*
- *1/4 teaspoon salt*
- *1 cup coconut milk*
- *1/2 cup water*
- *2 eggs*
- *1/2 teaspoon vanilla extract*
- *Butter or oil for greasing*
- *Toppings (choose from chocolate sprinkles, crushed peanuts, grated cheese, condensed milk, Nutella, etc.)*

Directions:

1. *In a bowl, whisk together all-purpose flour, granulated sugar, baking powder, and salt.*
2. *In another bowl, mix coconut milk, water, eggs, and vanilla extract until well combined.*
3. *Gradually pour the wet mixture into the dry ingredients, whisking until smooth and no lumps remain.*

4. *Heat a non-stick pan or skillet over medium heat and lightly grease it with butter or oil.*

5. *Pour a ladleful of the batter into the pan, spreading it evenly to form a thin pancake.*

6. *Cook for about 2-3 minutes until bubbles form on the surface and the edges start to lift.*

7. *Sprinkle your desired toppings over the pancake.*

8. *Carefully fold the pancake in half or quarters to enclose the toppings.*

9. *Cook for another 2-3 minutes until golden brown and cooked through.*

10. *Repeat with the remaining batter and toppings.*

11. *Slice the Martabak Manis into pieces and serve warm.*

Bakwan Sayur (Vegetable Fritters)

Servings: 4 Time: 30 minutes

Ingredients:

- *1 cup all-purpose flour*
- *1/4 cup rice flour*
- *1 teaspoon baking powder*
- *1/2 teaspoon ground turmeric*
- *1/2 teaspoon salt*
- *1/4 teaspoon ground white pepper*
- *1 cup water*
- *1 carrot, julienned*
- *1 small cabbage, thinly sliced*
- *1/2 cup bean sprouts*
- *2 scallions, chopped*
- *Oil for deep frying*

Directions:

1. *In a large mixing bowl, combine all-purpose flour, rice flour, baking powder, ground turmeric, salt, and ground white pepper.*
2. *Gradually add water to the dry ingredients, whisking until you get a smooth batter without lumps.*

3. Add julienned carrot, thinly sliced cabbage, bean sprouts, and chopped scallions to the batter. Mix well to coat the vegetables evenly.

4. Heat oil in a deep frying pan or pot over medium-high heat.

5. Drop spoonfuls of the vegetable batter into the hot oil, making sure not to overcrowd the pan.

6. Fry the fritters for about 3-4 minutes until golden brown and crispy, turning them occasionally for even cooking.

7. Remove the fritters from the oil using a slotted spoon and drain them on paper towels to remove excess oil.

8. Repeat the frying process with the remaining batter and vegetables.

9. Serve the Bakwan Sayur hot with a dipping sauce of your choice, such as sweet chili sauce or soy sauce with chopped chili.

Perkedel Kentang (Potato Fritters)

Servings: 4 Time: 30 minutes

Ingredients:

- *4 medium potatoes, peeled and boiled*
- *1 egg, beaten*
- *2 tablespoons all-purpose flour*
- *1/2 teaspoon ground white pepper*
- *1/2 teaspoon salt, or to taste*
- *2 cloves garlic, minced*
- *2 tablespoons chopped scallions*
- *Oil for frying*

Directions:

1. *Mash the boiled potatoes in a mixing bowl until smooth and lump-free.*
2. *Add beaten egg, all-purpose flour, ground white pepper, salt, minced garlic, and chopped scallions to the mashed potatoes. Mix well to combine all ingredients thoroughly.*
3. *Heat oil in a frying pan over medium heat.*
4. *Take a spoonful of the potato mixture and shape it into a small patty or ball.*

5. *Carefully place the potato patty into the hot oil, flattening it slightly with a spatula.*

6. *Fry the perkedel until golden brown and crispy on both sides, about 3-4 minutes per side.*

7. *Remove the perkedel from the oil and drain excess oil on paper towels.*

8. *Repeat the frying process with the remaining potato mixture.*

Otak-Otak (Fish Cake)

Servings: 4 Time: 45 minutes

Ingredients:

- *500g white fish fillets (such as tilapia or cod)*
- *1 tablespoon oil*
- *2 cloves garlic, minced*
- *1 onion, finely chopped*
- *2 tablespoons coconut milk*
- *1 tablespoon fish sauce*
- *1 teaspoon sugar*
- *1 teaspoon ground turmeric*
- *1 teaspoon ground coriander*
- *1 teaspoon ground cumin*
- *1/2 teaspoon chili powder (optional, for spiciness)*
- *Salt and pepper to taste*
- *Banana leaves or aluminum foil for wrapping*

Directions:

1. *Rinse the fish fillets and pat them dry with paper towels. Cut the fish into small chunks.*
2. *Heat oil in a pan over medium heat. Add minced garlic and chopped onion, and sauté until fragrant.*

3. Add the fish chunks to the pan and cook until they are cooked through and easily flaked with a fork.

4. In a blender or food processor, combine the cooked fish, coconut milk, fish sauce, sugar, ground turmeric, ground coriander, ground cumin, chili powder (if using), salt, and pepper. Blend until you get a smooth paste.

5. Preheat your grill or oven to medium-high heat.

6. Cut banana leaves or aluminum foil into squares for wrapping the fish mixture.

7. Place a spoonful of the fish mixture onto each banana leaf or foil square and fold it to form a packet, securing the edges with toothpicks or string.

8. Grill or bake the Otak-Otak packets for about 15-20 minutes until the fish mixture is cooked and the banana leaves or foil are slightly charred.

9. Remove from heat and carefully open the packets.

10. Serve the Otak-Otak hot with steamed rice and a side of sambal or dipping sauce.

Pempek Palembang (Fish Cake from Palembang)

Servings: 4 Time: 1 hour

Ingredients: For the Fish Cake:

- *500g white fish fillets (such as mackerel or tilapia), deboned*
- *100g tapioca flour*
- *2 cloves garlic, minced*
- *1 egg*
- *1 teaspoon salt*
- *1/2 teaspoon sugar*
- *1/2 teaspoon ground white pepper*
- *Oil for frying*

For the Sauce (Cuko):

- *200ml water*
- *100g palm sugar or brown sugar*
- *3 tablespoons tamarind juice (strained)*
- *1 teaspoon salt*
- *2 red chilies, finely chopped*
- *2 cloves garlic, minced*
- *1/2 teaspoon ground white pepper*

- *1/2 teaspoon ground coriander*
- *1/2 teaspoon cornstarch (optional, for thickening)*

Directions:

1. *In a blender or food processor, combine the deboned fish fillets, tapioca flour, minced garlic, egg, salt, sugar, and ground white pepper. Blend until you get a smooth and sticky fish paste.*
2. *Wet your hands with water and shape the fish paste into oval or rectangular patties.*
3. *Heat oil in a frying pan over medium heat.*
4. *Fry the fish cakes in hot oil until golden brown and cooked through, about 5-7 minutes per side. Drain excess oil on paper towels.*
5. *For the sauce (cuko), combine water, palm sugar or brown sugar, tamarind juice, salt, chopped red chilies, minced garlic, ground white pepper, and ground coriander in a saucepan. Bring to a simmer over medium heat, stirring until the sugar is dissolved.*
6. *If desired, mix cornstarch with a little water to make a slurry and add it to the sauce to thicken it. Stir well.*
7. *Remove the sauce from heat and let it cool slightly before serving.*

8. *Serve the Pempek Palembang hot with the spicy sauce (cuko) on the side for dipping.*

Sayur Asem (Tamarind Vegetable Soup)

Servings: 4 Time: 45 minutes

Ingredients:

- *1 liter water*
- *200g pumpkin, cut into chunks*
- *1 tomato, quartered*
- *1 corn on the cob, cut into pieces*
- *100g chayote squash, peeled and sliced*
- *100g green beans, trimmed and cut into bite-sized pieces*
- *2 red chilies, sliced*
- *2 bay leaves*
- *2 tablespoons tamarind paste (dissolved in 1/4 cup warm water, strained)*
- *2 tablespoons palm sugar or brown sugar*
- *Salt to taste*
- *Fried shallots for garnish (optional)*

Directions:

1. *In a large pot, bring water to a boil.*
2. *Add pumpkin chunks, quartered tomato, corn pieces, sliced chayote squash, green beans, sliced red chilies, and bay leaves to the boiling water.*

3. *Simmer the vegetables over medium heat until they are tender but not mushy, about 15-20 minutes.*

4. *Stir in the dissolved tamarind paste (strained), palm sugar or brown sugar, and salt to taste. Adjust the sweetness and sourness according to your preference by adding more sugar or tamarind paste if needed.*

5. *Let the soup simmer for another 5 minutes to allow the flavors to meld.*

6. *Remove the bay leaves from the soup.*

7. *Serve the Sayur Asem hot in bowls, garnished with fried shallots if desired.*

Rujak Buah (Fruit Salad with Spicy Dressing)

Servings: 4 Time: 20 minutes

Ingredients: For the Spicy Dressing (Bumbu Rujak):

- *3 red chilies, seeded and chopped*
- *2 cloves garlic*
- *1 tablespoon palm sugar or brown sugar*
- *1 tablespoon tamarind paste (dissolved in 2 tablespoons warm water, strained)*
- *1 teaspoon shrimp paste (terasi), roasted*
- *Salt to taste*

For the Fruit Salad:

- *1 cucumber, peeled and sliced*
- *1 green apple, julienned*
- *1 ripe mango, peeled and sliced*
- *1 papaya, peeled and sliced*
- *1 pineapple, peeled and sliced*
- *1 jicama (singkong), peeled and sliced (optional)*
- *1 firm banana, sliced (optional)*
- *1 handful roasted peanuts, crushed (for garnish)*
- *1 handful fried shallots (optional, for garnish)*

Directions:

1. *To make the spicy dressing (bumbu rujak), blend red chilies, garlic, palm sugar or brown sugar, tamarind paste (strained), roasted shrimp paste, and salt in a blender or food processor until you get a smooth paste. Adjust the sweetness, sourness, and spiciness according to your taste.*

2. *In a large mixing bowl, combine sliced cucumber, julienned green apple, sliced ripe mango, sliced papaya, sliced pineapple, jicama (if using), and sliced banana (if using).*

3. *Pour the spicy dressing (bumbu rujak) over the mixed fruits and toss well to coat the fruits evenly with the dressing.*

4. *Transfer the fruit salad to serving plates or bowls.*

5. *Garnish the Rujak Buah with crushed roasted peanuts and fried shallots for added flavor and texture.*

MAIN COURSES - VEGETARIAN

Nasi Goreng (Fried Rice)

Servings: 4 Time: 30 minutes

Ingredients:

- *4 cups cooked white rice (preferably leftover rice)*
- *2 tablespoons oil (vegetable or canola oil)*
- *2 cloves garlic, minced*
- *1 onion, finely chopped*

- *2 eggs, beaten*
- *200g mixed vegetables (such as carrots, peas, corn)*
- *200g tofu or tempeh, diced*
- *2 tablespoons soy sauce*
- *1 tablespoon sweet soy sauce (kecap manis)*
- *1 teaspoon shrimp paste (terasi), optional*
- *Salt and pepper to taste*
- *Sliced cucumber and tomato for garnish*
- *Fried shallots for garnish*

Directions:

1. *Heat oil in a large pan or wok over medium heat.*
2. *Add minced garlic and chopped onion to the pan. Sauté until fragrant and onions are translucent.*
3. *Push the garlic and onion to one side of the pan and pour the beaten eggs into the empty space. Scramble the eggs until they are cooked through.*
4. *Add diced tofu or tempeh to the pan and stir-fry until lightly browned.*
5. *Add mixed vegetables to the pan and stir-fry for a few minutes until they are tender but still crisp.*
6. *Add cooked white rice to the pan, breaking up any clumps with a spatula. Stir-fry everything together for a few minutes to mix well.*

7. Season the fried rice with soy sauce, sweet soy sauce (kecap manis), shrimp paste (if using), salt, and pepper. Adjust the seasoning according to your taste.

8. Continue stir-frying the fried rice until everything is evenly coated and heated through.

9. Remove the pan from heat and transfer the Nasi Goreng to serving plates.

10. Garnish with sliced cucumber, tomato, and fried shallots.

Gado-Gado (Vegetable Salad with Peanut Sauce)

Servings: 4 Time: 30 minutes

Ingredients: For the Peanut Sauce:

- *1 cup roasted peanuts, finely ground*
- *2 cloves garlic, minced*
- *1 small onion, finely chopped*
- *2 tablespoons tamarind paste (dissolved in 1/4 cup warm water, strained)*
- *2 tablespoons palm sugar or brown sugar*
- *1 teaspoon shrimp paste (terasi), roasted*
- *1/2 cup coconut milk*
- *Salt to taste*
- *Water (as needed for desired consistency)*

For the Salad:

- *4 cups mixed vegetables (such as blanched green beans, boiled potatoes, boiled carrots, bean sprouts, cabbage, cucumber, and tofu)*
- *Hard-boiled eggs, halved*
- *Fried tempeh or tofu, sliced*
- *Fried shallots for garnish*

Directions:

1. *In a blender or food processor, combine finely ground roasted peanuts, minced garlic, chopped onion, tamarind paste (strained), palm sugar or brown sugar, roasted shrimp paste, coconut milk, and salt. Blend until you get a smooth and creamy peanut sauce. Add water as needed to adjust the consistency.*

2. *Arrange the mixed vegetables, hard-boiled eggs, fried tempeh or tofu on serving plates or a large serving platter.*

3. *Drizzle the prepared peanut sauce generously over the vegetables, eggs, and tofu/tempeh.*

4. *Garnish the Gado-Gado with fried shallots for added flavor and texture.*

5. *Serve the Gado-Gado immediately, allowing each person to mix the peanut sauce with the vegetables and other components before enjoying.*

Tempeh Goreng (Fried Tempeh)

Servings: 4 Time: 20 minutes

Ingredients:

- *250g tempeh, sliced into thin rectangles or triangles*
- *Oil for frying*
- *2 cloves garlic, minced*
- *1 red chili, sliced (optional for spiciness)*
- *Salt to taste*
- *Lime wedges for serving*

Directions:

1. *Heat oil in a frying pan or skillet over medium-high heat.*
2. *Add minced garlic and sliced red chili (if using) to the hot oil. Sauté until fragrant.*
3. *Add the sliced tempeh to the pan in a single layer. Fry until golden brown and crispy on both sides, about 3-4 minutes per side.*
4. *Use a slotted spoon to transfer the fried tempeh to a plate lined with paper towels to drain excess oil.*
5. *Sprinkle salt over the hot fried tempeh, adjusting the amount according to your taste.*

6. *Serve the Tempeh Goreng hot with lime wedges on the side for squeezing over the tempeh before eating.*

Sayur Lodeh (Vegetable Stew in Coconut Milk)

Servings: 4 Time: 30 minutes

Ingredients:

- *1 cup coconut milk*
- *2 cups water or vegetable broth*
- *200g tofu, diced*
- *1 cup green beans, cut into 2-inch pieces*
- *1 carrot, sliced*
- *1 small eggplant, sliced*
- *1 cup cabbage, chopped*
- *1 handful bean sprouts*
- *2 kaffir lime leaves*
- *2 bay leaves*
- *2 cloves garlic, minced*
- *1 onion, finely chopped*
- *2 red chilies, sliced (optional for spiciness)*
- *1 teaspoon ground turmeric*
- *1 teaspoon ground coriander*
- *Salt and sugar to taste*
- *Oil for cooking*

Directions:

1. Heat oil in a large pot or pan over medium heat.
2. Add minced garlic, chopped onion, and sliced red chilies (if using). Sauté until fragrant.
3. Add diced tofu to the pot and cook until lightly browned.
4. Stir in ground turmeric and ground coriander, and cook for another minute to toast the spices.
5. Pour coconut milk and water or vegetable broth into the pot. Stir well to combine.
6. Add kaffir lime leaves and bay leaves to the pot.
7. Bring the coconut milk mixture to a simmer.
8. Add green beans, sliced carrot, sliced eggplant, chopped cabbage, and bean sprouts to the pot. Stir gently to mix the vegetables with the coconut milk.
9. Season the Sayur Lodeh with salt and sugar to taste. Adjust the seasoning according to your preference.
10. Let the stew simmer for about 10-15 minutes until the vegetables are tender but still retain some crispness.
11. Remove the kaffir lime leaves and bay leaves from the stew before serving.

Tahu Tek-Tek (Crispy Tofu with Peanut Sauce)

Servings: 4 Time: 30 minutes

Ingredients: For the Crispy Tofu:

- *400g firm tofu, cut into cubes*
- *Oil for frying*

For the Peanut Sauce:

- *1 cup roasted peanuts, finely ground*
- *2 cloves garlic, minced*
- *1 small onion, finely chopped*
- *2 tablespoons tamarind paste (dissolved in 1/4 cup warm water, strained)*
- *2 tablespoons palm sugar or brown sugar*
- *1 teaspoon shrimp paste (terasi), roasted*
- *1/2 cup coconut milk*
- *Salt to taste*
- *Water (as needed for desired consistency)*

For Serving:

- *Sliced cucumber and tomato*

- *Fried shallots for garnish*

Directions:

1. *Heat oil in a frying pan or skillet over medium-high heat.*

2. *Fry the tofu cubes in hot oil until golden brown and crispy on all sides. Use a slotted spoon to transfer the fried tofu to a plate lined with paper towels to drain excess oil.*

3. *In a blender or food processor, combine finely ground roasted peanuts, minced garlic, chopped onion, tamarind paste (strained), palm sugar or brown sugar, roasted shrimp paste, coconut milk, and salt. Blend until you get a smooth and creamy peanut sauce. Add water as needed to adjust the consistency.*

4. *Arrange the fried tofu cubes on serving plates.*

5. *Drizzle the prepared peanut sauce generously over the fried tofu.*

6. *Garnish with sliced cucumber, tomato, and fried shallots.*

7. *Serve the Tahu Tek-Tek immediately, allowing each person to mix the peanut sauce with the crispy tofu before enjoying.*

Pecel Lele (Fried Catfish with Spicy Sauce)

Servings: 4 Time: 40 minutes

Ingredients: For the Fried Catfish:

- *4 catfish fillets*
- *1 teaspoon turmeric powder*
- *Salt to taste*
- *Oil for frying*

For the Spicy Sauce (Sambal):

- *6 red chilies, seeded and chopped*
- *4 cloves garlic*
- *2 shallots, chopped*
- *1 tablespoon tamarind paste (dissolved in 2 tablespoons warm water, strained)*
- *1 tablespoon palm sugar or brown sugar*
- *Salt to taste*
- *Water (as needed for desired consistency)*

For Serving:

- *Cooked rice*
- *Cucumber and tomato slices*
- *Fried shallots for garnish*

Directions:

1. Marinate the catfish fillets with turmeric powder and salt. Let them marinate for about 15-20 minutes.
2. Heat oil in a frying pan or skillet over medium heat.
3. Fry the marinated catfish fillets in hot oil until golden brown and crispy on both sides. Use a slotted spoon to transfer the fried catfish to a plate lined with paper towels to drain excess oil.
4. In a blender or food processor, combine chopped red chilies, garlic, shallots, tamarind paste (strained), palm sugar or brown sugar, and salt. Blend until you get a smooth and spicy sauce (sambal). Add water as needed to adjust the consistency.
5. Arrange the fried catfish fillets on serving plates.
6. Drizzle the prepared spicy sauce (sambal) over the fried catfish.
7. Garnish with cucumber and tomato slices, and fried shallots.
8. Serve the Pecel Lele hot with cooked rice on the side.

Nasi Campur Bali (Balinese Mixed Rice)

Servings: 4 Time: 45 minutes

Ingredients: For the Base Rice:

- *2 cups cooked white rice (preferably jasmine rice)*

For the Spiced Minced Chicken (Ayam Betutu):

- *300g minced chicken*
- *2 tablespoons Balinese spice paste (Basa Genap)*
- *2 tablespoons oil*
- *Salt to taste*

For the Spicy Shredded Chicken (Ayam Sisit):

- *300g chicken breast, boiled and shredded*
- *2 tablespoons Balinese spice paste (Basa Genap)*
- *2 tablespoons oil*
- *Salt to taste*

For the Sate Lilit (Balinese Fish Satay):

- *300g white fish fillets (such as snapper or mackerel)*
- *2 tablespoons Balinese spice paste (Basa Genap)*
- *2 tablespoons grated coconut (fresh or desiccated)*
- *Bamboo skewers (for grilling)*

For the Accompaniments:

- *Sambal Matah (Balinese raw chili sambal)*
- *Fried shallots*
- *Boiled egg, halved*
- *Steamed vegetables (such as long beans, bean sprouts, and spinach)*

Directions:

1. *Prepare the Base Rice:*
   - *Cook white rice according to package instructions. Keep it warm.*
2. *Prepare the Spiced Minced Chicken (Ayam Betutu):*
   - *In a pan, heat oil over medium heat. Add Balinese spice paste and sauté until fragrant.*
   - *Add minced chicken to the pan and cook until cooked through. Season with salt to taste.*
3. *Prepare the Spicy Shredded Chicken (Ayam Sisit):*
   - *Heat oil in a separate pan over medium heat. Add Balinese spice paste and sauté until aromatic.*
   - *Add shredded chicken to the pan and stir-fry until coated with the spice paste. Season with salt to taste.*
4. *Prepare the Sate Lilit (Balinese Fish Satay):*
   - *In a bowl, mix Balinese spice paste with grated coconut to form a paste.*

- o *Cut fish fillets into small pieces and mix with the spice paste mixture.*
- o *Thread the fish mixture onto bamboo skewers to form satay.*
- o *Grill the satay skewers over medium-high heat until cooked and slightly charred.*

5. *Assemble the Nasi Campur Bali:*
   - o *Place a portion of the cooked white rice in the center of each serving plate.*
   - o *Arrange the Spiced Minced Chicken (Ayam Betutu), Spicy Shredded Chicken (Ayam Sisit), and Sate Lilit (Balinese Fish Satay) around the rice.*
   - o *Add a dollop of Sambal Matah on the side of the plate.*
   - o *Garnish with fried shallots, boiled egg halves, and steamed vegetables.*

Tumis Kangkung (Stir-Fried Water Spinach)

Servings: 4 Time: 15 minutes

Ingredients:

- *500g water spinach (kangkung), washed and trimmed*
- *2 tablespoons oil (vegetable or canola oil)*
- *3 cloves garlic, minced*
- *2 red chilies, sliced (optional for spiciness)*
- *1 teaspoon shrimp paste (terasi), roasted*
- *1 tablespoon oyster sauce*
- *Salt and pepper to taste*

Directions:

1. *Heat oil in a wok or large pan over medium-high heat.*
2. *Add minced garlic and sliced red chilies (if using) to the hot oil. Sauté until fragrant.*
3. *Add roasted shrimp paste (terasi) to the pan and stir-fry for a few seconds to release its aroma.*
4. *Add water spinach (kangkung) to the pan. Stir-fry quickly to coat the spinach with the garlic and shrimp paste mixture.*

5. *Add oyster sauce to the pan and continue stir-frying for another minute or until the water spinach is wilted but still vibrant green.*

6. *Season with salt and pepper to taste. Be careful with salt as the oyster sauce is already salty.*

7. *Remove the Tumis Kangkung from heat and transfer to a serving dish.*

Nasi Padang (Padang Rice with Assorted Dishes)

Ingredients:

- *Cooked white rice (steamed)*
- *Rendang (Indonesian Spicy Beef Stew)*
- *Ayam Goreng (Fried Chicken)*
- *Sambal (Spicy Chili Sauce)*
- *Balado Telur (Spicy Eggs)*
- *Gulai Cubadak (Young Jackfruit Curry)*
- *Sayur Lodeh (Vegetable Stew in Coconut Milk)*
- *Kerupuk (Indonesian Crackers)*
- *Sliced cucumber and tomato (for garnish)*

Instructions:

1. *Prepare the individual dishes:*
   - *Cook Rendang (Indonesian Spicy Beef Stew) until tender and flavorful.*
   - *Fry Ayam Goreng (Fried Chicken) until golden and crispy.*
   - *Make Sambal (Spicy Chili Sauce) by blending red chilies, garlic, shallots, tomato, and shrimp paste. Sauté the mixture until fragrant.*

- o *Prepare Balado Telur (Spicy Eggs) by boiling eggs, peeling them, and then frying in a spicy chili sauce.*

- o *Cook Gulai Cubadak (Young Jackfruit Curry) until the jackfruit is tender and infused with the curry flavors.*

- o *Make Sayur Lodeh (Vegetable Stew in Coconut Milk) with mixed vegetables cooked in coconut milk and spices.*

- o *Serve Kerupuk (Indonesian Crackers) as a crunchy accompaniment.*

2. *Arrange the dishes on a large serving platter or individual plates, placing each dish neatly around a mound of steamed white rice.*

3. *Garnish with sliced cucumber and tomato for freshness and color.*

4. *Serve the Nasi Padang hot, allowing diners to mix and match the dishes with the rice and sambal according to their preferences.*

Sambal Goreng Tempeh (Spicy Fried Tempeh)

Servings: 4 Time: 30 minutes

Ingredients:

- *300g tempeh, cut into cubes or strips*
- *Oil for frying*
- *3 tablespoons oil (vegetable or canola oil)*
- *2 cloves garlic, minced*
- *1 onion, finely chopped*
- *2 red chilies, sliced (adjust to taste)*
- *2 tomatoes, chopped*
- *1 teaspoon shrimp paste (terasi), roasted*
- *1 tablespoon sweet soy sauce (kecap manis)*
- *Salt to taste*
- *Sugar to taste (optional)*
- *Lime wedges for serving*

Directions:

1. *Heat oil in a frying pan or skillet over medium-high heat.*
2. *Fry the tempeh cubes or strips in hot oil until golden brown and crispy. Use a slotted spoon to transfer the fried*

tempeh to a plate lined with paper towels to drain excess oil.

3. In a separate pan, heat 3 tablespoons of oil over medium heat.

4. Add minced garlic, chopped onion, and sliced red chilies to the hot oil. Sauté until fragrant and onions are translucent.

5. Add chopped tomatoes to the pan and cook until they soften and release their juices.

6. Add roasted shrimp paste (terasi) to the pan and stir-fry for a minute to combine.

7. Add fried tempeh to the pan and mix well with the tomato and spice mixture.

8. Stir in sweet soy sauce (kecap manis) and season with salt to taste. You can also add sugar if desired for a touch of sweetness.

9. Cook the Sambal Goreng Tempeh for a few more minutes until the flavors are well combined and the tempeh is coated with the sauce.

10. Remove from heat and transfer the Sambal Goreng Tempeh to a serving dish.

11. Serve hot with steamed white rice and lime wedges on the side for squeezing over the tempeh before eating.

MAIN COURSES - SEAFOOD

Ikan Bakar (Grilled Fish)

Servings: 4 Time: 30 minutes

Ingredients:

- *4 fish fillets (such as snapper, tilapia, or mackerel)*
- *4 tablespoons soy sauce*
- *2 tablespoons sweet soy sauce (kecap manis)*
- *2 tablespoons lime juice*

- *2 cloves garlic, minced*
- *1 teaspoon ground turmeric*
- *1 teaspoon ground coriander*
- *1 teaspoon ground cumin*
- *1 teaspoon brown sugar*
- *Salt to taste*
- *Oil for grilling*
- *Sliced lime and fresh cilantro for garnish*

Directions:

1. *In a bowl, mix together soy sauce, sweet soy sauce (kecap manis), lime juice, minced garlic, ground turmeric, ground coriander, ground cumin, brown sugar, and salt to create a marinade.*

2. *Pat the fish fillets dry with paper towels and then coat them evenly with the marinade. Let the fish marinate for at least 15-20 minutes in the refrigerator.*

3. *Preheat your grill to medium-high heat. Brush the grill grates with oil to prevent sticking.*

4. *Place the marinated fish fillets on the grill and cook for about 5-7 minutes per side or until the fish is cooked through and has nice grill marks.*

5. *While grilling, baste the fish occasionally with the remaining marinade to keep it moist and flavorful.*

6. *Once the fish is cooked and has a nice charred exterior, remove it from the grill and transfer to a serving plate.*

7. *Garnish the Ikan Bakar with sliced lime and fresh cilantro.*

8. *Serve hot with steamed rice and your favorite side dishes.*

Udang Goreng Tepung (Fried Shrimp with Crispy Batter)

Servings: 4 Time: 30 minutes

Ingredients:

- *500g large shrimp, peeled and deveined*
- *Oil for frying*

For the Batter:

- *1 cup all-purpose flour*
- *1/2 cup cornstarch*
- *1 teaspoon baking powder*
- *1 teaspoon salt*
- *1/2 teaspoon ground black pepper*
- *1 egg*
- *1 cup cold water*

For the Dipping Sauce (optional):

- *Sweet chili sauce or cocktail sauce*

Directions:

1. In a bowl, combine all-purpose flour, cornstarch, baking powder, salt, and ground black pepper to make the batter.

2. In a separate bowl, beat the egg and then gradually add cold water while stirring to create a smooth batter.

3. Heat oil in a deep fryer or deep frying pan to 350°F (175°C).

4. Dip each shrimp into the batter, making sure it's evenly coated.

5. Carefully place the battered shrimp into the hot oil and fry in batches for about 2-3 minutes or until golden brown and crispy.

6. Use a slotted spoon to remove the fried shrimp from the oil and place them on a plate lined with paper towels to drain excess oil.

7. Repeat the frying process with the remaining shrimp and batter.

8. Serve the Udang Goreng Tepung hot with sweet chili sauce or cocktail sauce on the side for dipping.

Pepes Ikan (Steamed Fish in Banana Leaf)

Servings: 4 Time: 45 minutes

Ingredients:

- *4 fish fillets (such as tilapia, snapper, or mackerel)*
- *Banana leaves (cut into squares, for wrapping)*
- *2 tomatoes, sliced*
- *1 onion, sliced*
- *2 stalks lemongrass, white part only, bruised*
- *4 kaffir lime leaves*
- *2 tablespoons tamarind juice (strained)*
- *Salt to taste*
- *Banana leaf strips or kitchen twine (for securing the parcels)*

For the Spice Paste (Basa Genap):

- *5 shallots*
- *3 cloves garlic*
- *3 red chilies (adjust to taste)*
- *1 inch ginger*
- *1 inch galangal*
- *1 teaspoon ground turmeric*
- *1 teaspoon shrimp paste (terasi), roasted*

49

Directions:

1. *Prepare the Spice Paste (Basa Genap):*
   - *In a blender or food processor, blend together shallots, garlic, red chilies, ginger, galangal, ground turmeric, and roasted shrimp paste until smooth.*
2. *Marinate the Fish:*
   - *Rub the fish fillets with tamarind juice and salt. Let them marinate for about 15-20 minutes.*
3. *Assemble the Pepes Ikan:*
   - *Take a piece of banana leaf and place a slice of tomato and onion in the center.*
   - *Place a marinated fish fillet on top of the tomato and onion slices.*
   - *Spread a generous amount of the Spice Paste (Basa Genap) over the fish fillet.*
   - *Add a stalk of bruised lemongrass and a kaffir lime leaf on top of the fish.*
4. *Fold and Secure the Parcels:*
   - *Fold the banana leaf to encase the fish and spices, creating a parcel.*
   - *Secure the parcel with banana leaf strips or kitchen twine.*
5. *Steam the Pepes Ikan:*

- o *Place the prepared Pepes Ikan parcels in a steamer basket.*

- o *Steam the parcels over medium-high heat for about 20-25 minutes or until the fish is cooked through and tender.*

6. *Serve:*

   - o *Carefully open the banana leaf parcels and transfer the steamed fish to serving plates.*

   - o *Serve the Pepes Ikan hot with steamed rice and sambal on the side.*

Cumi Goreng Tepung (Fried Calamari with Crispy Batter)

Servings: 4 Time: 30 minutes

Ingredients:

- *500g calamari (squid), cleaned and cut into rings*
- *Oil for frying*

For the Batter:

- *1 cup all-purpose flour*
- *1/2 cup cornstarch*
- *1 teaspoon baking powder*
- *1 teaspoon salt*
- *1/2 teaspoon ground black pepper*
- *1 egg*
- *1 cup cold water*

For the Dipping Sauce (optional):

- *Aioli sauce or marinara sauce*

Directions:

1. *In a bowl, combine all-purpose flour, cornstarch, baking powder, salt, and ground black pepper to make the batter.*

2. *In a separate bowl, beat the egg and then gradually add cold water while stirring to create a smooth batter.*

3. *Heat oil in a deep fryer or deep frying pan to 350°F (175°C).*

4. *Dip each calamari ring into the batter, making sure it's evenly coated.*

5. *Carefully place the battered calamari rings into the hot oil and fry in batches for about 2-3 minutes or until golden brown and crispy.*

6. *Use a slotted spoon to remove the fried calamari from the oil and place them on a plate lined with paper towels to drain excess oil.*

7. *Repeat the frying process with the remaining calamari rings and batter.*

8. *Serve the Cumi Goreng Tepung hot with aioli sauce or marinara sauce on the side for dipping.*

Pindang Serani (Sour and Spicy Fish Soup)

Servings: 4 Time: 40 minutes

Ingredients:

- *500g fish fillets (such as mackerel or tilapia), cut into chunks*
- *1 onion, sliced*
- *2 tomatoes, chopped*
- *2 green chilies, sliced*
- *2 tablespoons tamarind paste (dissolved in 1/2 cup warm water, strained)*
- *1 tablespoon palm sugar or brown sugar*
- *Salt to taste*
- *2 cups water or fish stock*
- *Fresh cilantro leaves for garnish*

For the Spice Paste (Basa Genap):

- *4 shallots*
- *3 cloves garlic*
- *3 red chilies (adjust to taste)*
- *1 inch ginger*
- *1 inch galangal*
- *1 teaspoon ground turmeric*

- *1 teaspoon ground coriander*
- *1 teaspoon shrimp paste (terasi), roasted*

Directions:

1. *Prepare the Spice Paste (Basa Genap):*
   - *In a blender or food processor, blend together shallots, garlic, red chilies, ginger, galangal, ground turmeric, ground coriander, and roasted shrimp paste until smooth.*
2. *In a pot or deep pan, heat some oil over medium heat and sauté the sliced onion until translucent.*
3. *Add the Spice Paste (Basa Genap) to the pot and cook until fragrant.*
4. *Add chopped tomatoes and green chilies to the pot. Stir and cook until the tomatoes soften.*
5. *Pour in the tamarind water (strained) and fish stock or water. Bring the mixture to a simmer.*
6. *Add palm sugar or brown sugar to the soup and season with salt to taste. Adjust the sweetness and sourness according to your preference by adding more sugar or tamarind water if needed.*
7. *Gently add the fish chunks to the simmering soup. Cook for about 10-15 minutes or until the fish is cooked through and tender.*

8. *Taste the soup and adjust the seasoning if necessary.*

9. *Remove the Pindang Serani from heat and transfer it to serving bowls.*

10. *Garnish with fresh cilantro leaves before serving.*

Gulai Udang (Shrimp Curry)

Servings: 4 Time: 30 minutes

Ingredients:

- *500g large shrimp, peeled and deveined*
- *2 tablespoons oil*
- *1 onion, finely chopped*
- *2 cloves garlic, minced*
- *2 tomatoes, chopped*
- *1 tablespoon tamarind paste (dissolved in 1/2 cup warm water, strained)*
- *1 can (400ml) coconut milk*
- *1 teaspoon ground turmeric*
- *1 teaspoon ground coriander*
- *1 teaspoon ground cumin*
- *1 teaspoon chili powder (adjust to taste)*
- *Salt to taste*
- *Sugar to taste (optional)*
- *Fresh cilantro leaves for garnish*

Directions:

1. *Heat oil in a deep pan or wok over medium heat.*

2. *Add chopped onion and minced garlic to the hot oil. Sauté until the onions are soft and translucent.*

3. *Add chopped tomatoes to the pan and cook until they break down and become soft.*

4. *Stir in ground turmeric, ground coriander, ground cumin, and chili powder. Cook for a minute to toast the spices and release their flavors.*

5. *Pour in the tamarind water (strained) and coconut milk. Stir well to combine.*

6. *Bring the mixture to a simmer and let it cook for a few minutes to allow the flavors to meld together.*

7. *Add the peeled and deveined shrimp to the simmering curry. Cook for about 5-7 minutes or until the shrimp are cooked through and turn pink.*

8. *Season the Gulai Udang with salt and sugar to taste. Adjust the seasoning according to your preference.*

9. *Remove the curry from heat and transfer it to a serving dish.*

10. *Garnish with fresh cilantro leaves before serving.*

Kerang Saus Padang (Clams in Padang Sauce)

Servings: 4 Time: 30 minutes

Ingredients:

- *1 kg fresh clams, cleaned and scrubbed*
- *2 tablespoons oil*
- *1 onion, finely chopped*
- *2 cloves garlic, minced*
- *2 tomatoes, chopped*
- *2 green chilies, sliced (adjust to taste)*
- *1 tablespoon tamarind paste (dissolved in 1/2 cup warm water, strained)*
- *1 tablespoon sweet soy sauce (kecap manis)*
- *1 teaspoon shrimp paste (terasi), roasted*
- *Salt to taste*
- *Sugar to taste (optional)*
- *Fresh cilantro leaves for garnish*

Directions:

1. *Heat oil in a deep pan or wok over medium heat.*
2. *Add chopped onion and minced garlic to the hot oil. Sauté until the onions are soft and translucent.*

3. *Add chopped tomatoes and sliced green chilies to the pan. Cook until the tomatoes are soft and pulpy.*

4. *Stir in sweet soy sauce (kecap manis) and roasted shrimp paste (terasi). Mix well to combine the flavors.*

5. *Pour in the tamarind water (strained) and bring the sauce to a simmer.*

6. *Add the cleaned clams to the simmering sauce. Cover the pan with a lid and let the clams cook for about 5-7 minutes or until they open up.*

7. *Season the Kerang Saus Padang with salt and sugar to taste. Adjust the seasoning according to your preference.*

8. *Once the clams are cooked and have opened up, remove the pan from heat.*

9. *Transfer the Kerang Saus Padang to a serving dish.*

10. *Garnish with fresh cilantro leaves before serving.*

Sambal Udang (Spicy Shrimp)

Servings: 4 Time: 20 minutes

Ingredients:

- *500g large shrimp, peeled and deveined*
- *2 tablespoons oil*
- *1 onion, finely chopped*
- *3 cloves garlic, minced*
- *3 red chilies, sliced (adjust to taste)*
- *2 tomatoes, chopped*
- *1 tablespoon tamarind paste (dissolved in 1/2 cup warm water, strained)*
- *1 tablespoon sweet soy sauce (kecap manis)*
- *Salt to taste*
- *Sugar to taste (optional)*
- *Fresh cilantro leaves for garnish*

Directions:

1. *Heat oil in a deep pan or wok over medium heat.*
2. *Add chopped onion and minced garlic to the hot oil. Sauté until the onions are soft and translucent.*
3. *Add sliced red chilies to the pan. Cook for a minute to release their spiciness.*

4. Stir in chopped tomatoes and cook until they break down and become soft.

5. Pour in the tamarind water (strained) and sweet soy sauce (kecap manis). Mix well to combine.

6. Add the peeled and deveined shrimp to the pan. Stir-fry the shrimp until they turn pink and are cooked through.

7. Season the Sambal Udang with salt and sugar to taste. Adjust the seasoning according to your preference.

8. Once the shrimp are cooked and the sauce has thickened slightly, remove the pan from heat.

9. Transfer the Sambal Udang to a serving dish.

10. Garnish with fresh cilantro leaves before serving.

Kakap Merah Asam Manis (Sweet and Sour Red Snapper)

Servings: 4 Time: 30 minutes

Ingredients:

- *4 red snapper fillets (about 200g each), skin removed*
- *Salt and pepper to taste*
- *Cornstarch, for dusting*
- *Oil for frying*

For the Sweet and Sour Sauce:

- *1 onion, thinly sliced*
- *1 red bell pepper, thinly sliced*
- *1 green bell pepper, thinly sliced*
- *2 cloves garlic, minced*
- *1/4 cup tomato ketchup*
- *2 tablespoons sweet soy sauce (kecap manis)*
- *2 tablespoons vinegar*
- *2 tablespoons sugar*
- *1 tablespoon cornstarch (dissolved in 2 tablespoons water)*
- *1 cup water*
- *Salt to taste*
- *Oil for cooking*

Garnish:

- *Spring onions, chopped*
- *Sesame seeds (optional)*

Directions:

1. *Season the red snapper fillets with salt and pepper, then lightly dust them with cornstarch.*
2. *Heat oil in a frying pan over medium-high heat. Fry the red snapper fillets until golden and cooked through. Remove and set aside.*
3. *In the same pan, add a little more oil if needed. Sauté the minced garlic until fragrant.*
4. *Add sliced onion, red bell pepper, and green bell pepper to the pan. Stir-fry until the vegetables are slightly softened.*
5. *In a bowl, mix together tomato ketchup, sweet soy sauce (kecap manis), vinegar, sugar, dissolved cornstarch, water, and salt to make the sweet and sour sauce.*
6. *Pour the sweet and sour sauce into the pan with the vegetables. Stir well to combine.*
7. *Bring the sauce to a simmer and cook until it thickens and becomes glossy.*
8. *Return the fried red snapper fillets to the pan. Coat the fillets with the sweet and sour sauce.*

9. *Cook for another minute or until the fish is heated through and well coated with the sauce.*

10. *Garnish with chopped spring onions and sesame seeds (if using).*

11. *Serve the Kakap Merah Asam Manis hot with steamed rice.*

Lobster Saus Tiram (Lobster in Oyster Sauce)

Servings: 4 Time: 30 minutes

Ingredients:

- *2 lobsters (about 500g each), cleaned and halved lengthwise*
- *Salt and pepper to taste*
- *Cornstarch, for dusting*
- *Oil for frying*

For the Sauce:

- *2 tablespoons oyster sauce*
- *1 tablespoon soy sauce*
- *1 tablespoon sweet soy sauce (kecap manis)*
- *1 tablespoon honey or sugar*
- *1 tablespoon cornstarch (dissolved in 2 tablespoons water)*
- *1 cup chicken or vegetable broth*
- *2 cloves garlic, minced*
- *1 thumb-sized ginger, thinly sliced*
- *1 red chili, sliced (optional)*
- *Spring onions, chopped for garnish*

Directions:

1. *Season the lobster halves with salt and pepper, then lightly dust them with cornstarch.*
2. *Heat oil in a large pan or wok over medium-high heat. Fry the lobster halves until they turn pink and are cooked through. Remove and set aside.*
3. *In the same pan, add a little more oil if needed. Sauté minced garlic, ginger slices, and sliced red chili (if using) until fragrant.*
4. *In a bowl, mix together oyster sauce, soy sauce, sweet soy sauce (kecap manis), honey or sugar, dissolved cornstarch, and broth to make the sauce.*
5. *Pour the sauce mixture into the pan with the aromatics. Stir well to combine.*
6. *Bring the sauce to a simmer and cook until it thickens and becomes glossy.*
7. *Return the fried lobster halves to the pan. Coat the lobster with the oyster sauce mixture.*
8. *Cook for another minute or until the lobster is heated through and well coated with the sauce.*
9. *Garnish with chopped spring onions.*
10. *Serve the Lobster Saus Tiram hot with steamed rice or noodles.*

MAIN COURSES - MEAT

Ayam Goreng Kalasan (Kalasan Fried Chicken)

Servings: 4 Time: 1 hour (including marinating time)

Ingredients:

- *1 whole chicken, cut into pieces*
- *5 shallots, peeled*
- *3 cloves garlic, peeled*

- *2 candlenuts (kemiri)*
- *2 teaspoons coriander seeds*
- *1 teaspoon salt*
- *1 teaspoon sugar*
- *1 teaspoon turmeric powder*
- *1 tablespoon tamarind paste (dissolved in 2 tablespoons warm water, strained)*
- *2 bay leaves*
- *Oil for frying*

For the Seasoning Paste (Bumbu Halus):

- *Blend together shallots, garlic, candlenuts, coriander seeds, salt, sugar, and turmeric powder to make a smooth paste.*

For the Glaze (Saus Kalasan):

- *3 tablespoons sweet soy sauce (kecap manis)*
- *1 tablespoon tamarind water (strained)*
- *1 teaspoon palm sugar or brown sugar*
- *1 teaspoon salt*

Directions:

1. *Marinate the Chicken:*
   - *Rub the chicken pieces with the seasoning paste (Bumbu Halus), ensuring they are well coated. Let the*

chicken marinate for at least 30 minutes in the refrigerator.

2. *Prepare the Glaze (Saus Kalasan):*
   o *In a bowl, mix together sweet soy sauce (kecap manis), tamarind water, palm sugar or brown sugar, and salt to make the glaze.*

3. *Fry the Chicken:*
   o *Heat oil in a deep fryer or frying pan over medium-high heat.*
   o *Fry the marinated chicken pieces until they are golden brown and cooked through. Drain on paper towels to remove excess oil.*

4. *Glaze the Chicken:*
   o *In a separate pan, heat the glaze (Saus Kalasan) over low heat.*
   o *Add fried chicken pieces to the pan with the glaze, turning them to coat evenly. Let the chicken simmer in the glaze for a few minutes to absorb the flavors.*

5. *Serve:*
   o *Transfer the Ayam Goreng Kalasan to a serving plate.*
   o *Garnish with bay leaves for aroma and presentation.*
   o *Serve hot with steamed rice and your favorite side dishes.*

Rendang Daging (Beef Rendang)

Servings: 4 Time: 3-4 hours

Ingredients:

- *500g beef (such as chuck or brisket), cut into cubes*
- *2 cans (400ml each) coconut milk*
- *4 kaffir lime leaves*
- *2 stalks lemongrass, bruised*
- *1 turmeric leaf (optional), torn into pieces*
- *Oil for cooking*

For the Spice Paste (Rempah):

- *6 shallots, peeled*
- *4 cloves garlic, peeled*
- *3 red chilies (adjust to taste)*
- *2 thumb-sized ginger, peeled*
- *2 thumb-sized galangal, peeled*
- *1 tablespoon coriander seeds, toasted*
- *1 teaspoon cumin seeds, toasted*
- *1 teaspoon fennel seeds, toasted*
- *5-6 dried red chilies, soaked in hot water and drained*
- *1 tablespoon tamarind paste (dissolved in 1/2 cup warm water, strained)*

- *2 tablespoons palm sugar or brown sugar*
- *Salt to taste*

Directions:

1. *Prepare the Spice Paste (Rempah):*
   - *In a blender or food processor, blend together shallots, garlic, red chilies, ginger, galangal, toasted coriander seeds, toasted cumin seeds, toasted fennel seeds, and soaked dried red chilies until you get a smooth paste.*

2. *Cook the Beef:*
   - *Heat oil in a large pot or Dutch oven over medium heat. Add the spice paste (Rempah) and sauté until fragrant.*
   - *Add the beef cubes to the pot and cook until they are browned on all sides.*

3. *Add Coconut Milk and Aromatics:*
   - *Pour in the coconut milk, followed by kaffir lime leaves, bruised lemongrass, and torn turmeric leaf (if using). Stir to combine.*

4. *Simmer the Rendang:*
   - *Bring the mixture to a boil, then reduce the heat to low. Let the Rendang simmer uncovered, stirring occasionally, for 3-4 hours or until the beef is tender and the sauce has thickened.*

5. *Season and Finish:*

- o *Stir in the tamarind water (strained), palm sugar or brown sugar, and salt to taste. Adjust the seasoning according to your preference.*

- o *Continue simmering until the sauce reaches a rich and thick consistency, and the beef is fork-tender.*

6. *Serve:*

- o *Remove the kaffir lime leaves, bruised lemongrass, and turmeric leaf (if used) before serving.*

- o *Serve the Rendang Daging hot with steamed rice or coconut rice.*

Sate Padang (Padang Satay)

Servings: 4 Time: 1 hour (including marinating time)

Ingredients:

- *500g beef or chicken, cut into cubes*
- *Bamboo skewers, soaked in water*
- *Oil for grilling*

For the Marinade:

- *5 shallots, peeled*
- *3 cloves garlic, peeled*
- *2 thumb-sized ginger, peeled*
- *2 thumb-sized galangal, peeled*
- *2 lemongrass stalks, white part only, thinly sliced*
- *5-6 dried red chilies, soaked in hot water and drained*
- *1 teaspoon turmeric powder or 1 thumb-sized fresh turmeric, peeled*
- *1 tablespoon coriander seeds, toasted and ground*
- *1 teaspoon cumin seeds, toasted and ground*
- *1 teaspoon salt*
- *1 tablespoon palm sugar or brown sugar*
- *2 tablespoons coconut milk (optional)*
- *2 tablespoons vegetable oil*

For the Sauce (Kuah Kacang):

- *200g roasted peanuts, peeled and ground into a paste*
- *2 cups coconut milk*
- *2 kaffir lime leaves*
- *1 teaspoon tamarind paste (dissolved in 1/2 cup warm water, strained)*
- *1 teaspoon palm sugar or brown sugar*
- *Salt to taste*
- *1 tablespoon vegetable oil*

For Garnish:

- *Fried shallots*
- *Lime wedges*
- *Cucumber slices*

Directions:

1. *Prepare the Marinade:*
   - *In a blender or food processor, blend together shallots, garlic, ginger, galangal, lemongrass, soaked dried red chilies, turmeric, ground coriander seeds, ground cumin seeds, salt, palm sugar or brown sugar, coconut milk (if using), and vegetable oil until you get a smooth paste.*
2. *Marinate the Meat:*

- *Combine the meat cubes with the marinade in a bowl. Mix well to coat the meat evenly. Cover and refrigerate for at least 2 hours or overnight.*

3. *Prepare the Sauce (Kuah Kacang):*

   - *In a saucepan, heat vegetable oil over medium heat. Add the ground peanuts and sauté until fragrant.*

   - *Pour in the coconut milk and add kaffir lime leaves. Stir to combine.*

   - *Add tamarind water, palm sugar or brown sugar, and salt to the sauce. Simmer over low heat, stirring occasionally, until the sauce thickens. Remove from heat and set aside.*

4. *Skewer and Grill the Meat:*

   - *Thread marinated meat cubes onto soaked bamboo skewers.*

   - *Preheat the grill or grill pan over medium-high heat. Brush with oil.*

   - *Grill the skewered meat until cooked through and slightly charred on all sides, about 10-15 minutes, depending on the thickness of the meat.*

5. *Serve:*

   - *Arrange the grilled Sate Padang on a serving platter.*

   - *Serve with the prepared Sauce (Kuah Kacang) on the side.*

- *Garnish with fried shallots, lime wedges, and cucumber slices.*

Sop Buntut (Oxtail Soup)

Servings: 4 Time: 3-4 hours

Ingredients:

- *1 kg oxtail, cut into pieces*
- *2 liters water*
- *2 carrots, peeled and sliced*
- *2 potatoes, peeled and cubed*
- *1 onion, chopped*
- *3 cloves garlic, minced*
- *2 tomatoes, chopped*
- *2 bay leaves*
- *2 stalks lemongrass, bruised*
- *Salt and pepper to taste*
- *Oil for cooking*
- *Fried shallots for garnish*
- *Sliced green onions for garnish*
- *Sliced red chilies for garnish (optional)*
- *Lime wedges for serving*

Directions:

1. *Prepare the Oxtail:*

o *Rinse the oxtail pieces under cold water and pat them dry with paper towels.*

2. *Brown the Oxtail:*

   o *Heat oil in a large pot over medium-high heat. Add the oxtail pieces and brown them on all sides. Remove and set aside.*

3. *Sauté Aromatics:*

   o *In the same pot, add a little more oil if needed. Sauté chopped onion and minced garlic until fragrant and translucent.*

4. *Cook the Soup:*

   o *Return the browned oxtail pieces to the pot. Add water, chopped tomatoes, bay leaves, and bruised lemongrass stalks. Bring to a boil.*

   o *Reduce heat to low, cover, and simmer for about 2-3 hours or until the oxtail is tender and almost falling off the bone.*

5. *Add Vegetables:*

   o *Once the oxtail is tender, add sliced carrots and cubed potatoes to the soup. Simmer until the vegetables are cooked through, about 15-20 minutes.*

6. *Season the Soup:*

   o *Season the Sop Buntut with salt and pepper to taste. Adjust the seasoning according to your preference.*

7. *Serve:*

- o *Ladle the hot Sop Buntut into serving bowls.*

- o *Garnish with fried shallots, sliced green onions, and sliced red chilies (if using).*

- o *Serve with lime wedges on the side for squeezing over the soup.*

Ayam Taliwang (Grilled Chicken from Lombok)

Servings: 4 Time: 1 hour (including marinating time)

Ingredients:

- *1 whole chicken, cut into pieces*
- *Juice of 1 lime*
- *Salt to taste*
- *Banana leaves or aluminum foil for grilling*

For the Marinade:

- *5 shallots, peeled*
- *4 cloves garlic, peeled*
- *5 red bird's eye chilies (adjust to taste)*
- *2 tomatoes, chopped*
- *2 tablespoons sweet soy sauce (kecap manis)*
- *2 tablespoons tamarind water (strained)*
- *1 teaspoon shrimp paste (terasi), roasted*
- *1 teaspoon sugar*
- *1 teaspoon salt*

For Serving:

- *Sliced cucumber*
- *Sliced tomato*
- *Lime wedges*
- *Fried shallots (optional)*

Directions:

1. *Marinate the Chicken:*
   - *Rub the chicken pieces with lime juice and salt. Set aside while you prepare the marinade.*
2. *Prepare the Marinade:*
   - *In a blender or food processor, blend together shallots, garlic, red bird's eye chilies, chopped tomatoes, sweet soy sauce (kecap manis), tamarind water, roasted shrimp paste (terasi), sugar, and salt until you get a smooth paste.*
3. *Marinate the Chicken:*
   - *Coat the chicken pieces evenly with the marinade. Cover and refrigerate for at least 1 hour or overnight for the flavors to develop.*
4. *Grill the Chicken:*
   - *Preheat a grill or grill pan over medium-high heat.*
   - *Wrap each marinated chicken piece in banana leaves or aluminum foil to keep the moisture while grilling.*

- Grill the chicken pieces for about 15-20 minutes on each side or until they are cooked through and charred nicely.

5. Serve:

- Remove the chicken from the grill and unwrap from the banana leaves or foil.
- Serve the Ayam Taliwang hot with sliced cucumber, sliced tomato, lime wedges, and fried shallots (if using) on the side.

Dendeng Balado (Spicy Beef Jerky)

Servings: Makes about 4 servings Time: 2 hours marinating +
30 minutes cooking

Ingredients:

- *500g beef sirloin or flank steak, thinly sliced*
- *3 tablespoons tamarind juice (from tamarind pulp)*
- *2 tablespoons soy sauce*
- *2 tablespoons sweet soy sauce (kecap manis)*
- *1 tablespoon palm sugar (gula jawa), grated or chopped*
- *1 teaspoon salt*
- *Oil for frying*

For the Balado Spice Paste:

- *5-6 red chilies (adjust to taste), seeded and chopped*
- *3 shallots, chopped*
- *3 cloves garlic, chopped*
- *1 tomato, chopped*
- *1 teaspoon shrimp paste (terasi), toasted*
- *1/2 teaspoon ground coriander*
- *1/2 teaspoon ground cumin*
- *1/2 teaspoon turmeric powder*
- *1/2 teaspoon sugar*

- *Salt to taste*

Directions:

1. *Marinate the Beef:*
   - *In a bowl, combine the thinly sliced beef with tamarind juice, soy sauce, sweet soy sauce, grated palm sugar, and salt. Mix well to coat the beef slices evenly. Let it marinate for at least 2 hours or overnight in the refrigerator.*

2. *Prepare the Balado Spice Paste:*
   - *In a food processor or blender, combine the red chilies, shallots, garlic, tomato, shrimp paste, ground coriander, ground cumin, turmeric powder, sugar, and salt. Blend until you get a smooth paste.*

3. *Cook the Beef:*
   - *Heat some oil in a pan over medium heat. Add the marinated beef slices and cook until they are browned and slightly crispy on both sides. Remove the beef from the pan and set aside.*

4. *Make the Balado Sauce:*
   - *In the same pan, add a little more oil if needed. Add the blended Balado spice paste and sauté until fragrant and the oil starts to separate from the paste.*

5. *Combine Beef and Balado Sauce:*
   - *Return the cooked beef slices to the pan with the Balado sauce. Stir well to coat the beef with the spicy sauce.*

6. *Simmer and Serve:*
   - *Let the beef simmer in the Balado sauce for a few minutes to absorb the flavors.*
   - *Once the beef is heated through and well-coated with the sauce, remove from heat.*

7. *Serve Dendeng Balado:*
   - *Transfer the Dendeng Balado to a serving dish.*
   - *Serve hot with steamed rice or as a side dish. Optionally, garnish with fried shallots or chopped green onions before serving.*

Rawon (Beef Soup from East Java)

Servings: 4 Time: 2-3 hours

Ingredients:

- *500g beef (such as brisket or chuck), cut into cubes*
- *2 liters water*
- *2 kaffir lime leaves*
- *2 bay leaves*
- *2 stalks lemongrass, bruised*
- *3 tomatoes, quartered*
- *2 tablespoons tamarind paste (dissolved in 1 cup warm water, strained)*
- *3 tablespoons oil*
- *Salt to taste*
- *Sugar to taste*
- *Fried shallots for garnish*
- *Sliced green onions for garnish*
- *Sambal oelek or sliced red chilies (optional) for serving*

For the Spice Paste (Bumbu):

- *6 shallots, peeled*
- *4 cloves garlic, peeled*
- *2 thumb-sized ginger, peeled*

- *2 thumb-sized galangal, peeled*
- *5-6 dried red chilies, soaked in hot water and drained*
- *1 tablespoon coriander seeds, toasted and ground*
- *1 teaspoon cumin seeds, toasted and ground*
- *1 teaspoon turmeric powder or 1 thumb-sized fresh turmeric, peeled*
- *1 teaspoon shrimp paste (terasi), roasted*

Directions:

1. *Prepare the Spice Paste (Bumbu):*
   - *In a blender or food processor, blend together shallots, garlic, ginger, galangal, soaked dried red chilies, ground coriander seeds, ground cumin seeds, turmeric, and roasted shrimp paste (terasi) until you get a smooth paste.*
2. *Cook the Beef:*
   - *Heat oil in a large pot over medium-high heat. Add the spice paste (Bumbu) and sauté until fragrant.*
   - *Add the beef cubes to the pot and brown them on all sides.*
3. *Add Aromatics and Water:*
   - *Add kaffir lime leaves, bay leaves, bruised lemongrass stalks, and quartered tomatoes to the pot with the beef.*

o *Pour in the water and tamarind water (strained). Stir to combine.*

4. *Simmer the Rawon:*

   o *Bring the mixture to a boil, then reduce heat to low. Cover and simmer for about 2-3 hours or until the beef is tender and the flavors are well developed.*

5. *Season and Serve:*

   o *Season the Rawon with salt and sugar to taste. Adjust the seasoning according to your preference.*

   o *Remove kaffir lime leaves, bay leaves, and lemongrass stalks before serving.*

   o *Ladle the hot Rawon into serving bowls.*

   o *Garnish with fried shallots, sliced green onions, and sambal oelek or sliced red chilies (if using).*

   o *Serve the Rawon with steamed rice or ketupat (rice cake).*

Sate Kambing (Lamb Satay)

Servings: 4 Time: 1-2 hours (including marinating time)

Ingredients:

- *500g lamb meat (leg or shoulder), cut into cubes*
- *Bamboo skewers, soaked in water*
- *Oil for grilling*

For the Marinade:

- *3 shallots, peeled and chopped*
- *3 cloves garlic, peeled and minced*
- *2 tablespoons sweet soy sauce (kecap manis)*
- *1 tablespoon soy sauce*
- *1 tablespoon tamarind paste (dissolved in 2 tablespoons warm water, strained)*
- *1 teaspoon ground coriander*
- *1 teaspoon ground cumin*
- *1 teaspoon turmeric powder*
- *1 tablespoon brown sugar or palm sugar*
- *Salt to taste*
- *Pepper to taste*

For the Peanut Sauce (Sambal Kacang):

- *200g roasted peanuts, ground into a paste*
- *2 cloves garlic, minced*
- *2 shallots, minced*
- *2 red chilies, minced (adjust to taste)*
- *1 tablespoon tamarind paste (dissolved in 1/2 cup warm water, strained)*
- *1 tablespoon palm sugar or brown sugar*
- *Salt to taste*
- *Water as needed*

For Serving:

- *Sliced cucumber and red onion*
- *Lime wedges*
- *Indonesian rice cakes (ketupat) or steamed rice*

Directions:

1. *Marinate the Lamb:*
   - *In a bowl, combine chopped shallots, minced garlic, sweet soy sauce (kecap manis), soy sauce, tamarind water, ground coriander, ground cumin, turmeric powder, brown sugar or palm sugar, salt, and pepper to make the marinade.*

- o *Add the lamb cubes to the marinade and mix well to coat. Cover and refrigerate for at least 1 hour, preferably overnight.*

2. **Prepare the Peanut Sauce (Sambal Kacang):**
   - o *In a saucepan, heat a little oil over medium heat. Sauté minced garlic, minced shallots, and minced red chilies until fragrant.*
   - o *Add the ground peanuts and stir-fry for a few minutes.*
   - o *Pour in the tamarind water, palm sugar or brown sugar, and salt. Add water as needed to achieve a thick but pourable consistency. Simmer for a few more minutes, then remove from heat.*

3. **Skewer and Grill the Lamb:**
   - o *Thread the marinated lamb cubes onto soaked bamboo skewers.*
   - o *Preheat a grill or grill pan over medium-high heat. Brush with oil.*
   - o *Grill the skewered lamb until cooked through and slightly charred on all sides, about 10-15 minutes, depending on the thickness of the meat.*

4. **Serve:**
   - o *Arrange the Lamb Satay on a serving platter.*
   - o *Serve with the prepared Peanut Sauce (Sambal Kacang) on the side.*
   - o *Garnish with sliced cucumber and red onion.*

o   *Serve with lime wedges and Indonesian rice cakes (ketupat) or steamed rice.*

Gulai Kambing (Lamb Curry)

Servings: 4 Time: 2-3 hours

Ingredients:

- *500g lamb meat (leg or shoulder), cut into cubes*
- *2 tablespoons vegetable oil*
- *2 potatoes, peeled and cubed*
- *1 large onion, chopped*
- *4 cloves garlic, minced*
- *2 tomatoes, chopped*
- *2 cups coconut milk*
- *2 cups water*
- *2 bay leaves*
- *2 kaffir lime leaves*
- *Salt to taste*
- *Sugar to taste*

For the Spice Paste (Bumbu):

- *6 shallots, peeled and chopped*
- *4 cloves garlic, peeled and chopped*
- *2 thumb-sized ginger, peeled and chopped*
- *2 thumb-sized galangal, peeled and chopped*
- *4-6 red chilies (adjust to taste)*

- *1 tablespoon coriander seeds, toasted and ground*
- *1 teaspoon cumin seeds, toasted and ground*
- *1 teaspoon turmeric powder*
- *1 teaspoon shrimp paste (terasi), roasted*

For Garnish:

- *Fried shallots*
- *Sliced red chilies (optional)*
- *Chopped cilantro or parsley*

Directions:

1. *Prepare the Spice Paste (Bumbu):*
   - *In a blender or food processor, blend together shallots, garlic, ginger, galangal, red chilies, ground coriander seeds, ground cumin seeds, turmeric powder, and roasted shrimp paste (terasi) until you get a smooth paste.*
2. *Cook the Lamb:*
   - *Heat vegetable oil in a large pot or Dutch oven over medium heat. Add the minced garlic and chopped onion. Sauté until fragrant and translucent.*
   - *Add the spice paste (Bumbu) to the pot and sauté until aromatic.*
3. *Add Coconut Milk and Water:*

- o *Add the chopped tomatoes to the pot and cook until they soften.*
- o *Add the lamb cubes to the pot and stir to coat with the spice mixture.*
- o *Pour in the coconut milk and water. Stir well to combine.*

4. *Simmer the Curry:*
   - o *Add bay leaves and kaffir lime leaves to the pot. Season with salt and sugar to taste.*
   - o *Bring the curry to a boil, then reduce heat to low. Cover and simmer for about 1.5 to 2 hours or until the lamb is tender and the sauce has thickened.*

5. *Add Potatoes:*
   - o *Add the cubed potatoes to the curry and continue simmering until the potatoes are cooked through and tender.*

6. *Adjust Seasoning and Serve:*
   - o *Taste the Gulai Kambing and adjust the seasoning if needed, adding more salt or sugar according to your preference.*
   - o *Remove bay leaves and kaffir lime leaves before serving.*
   - o *Garnish the curry with fried shallots, sliced red chilies (if using), and chopped cilantro or parsley.*

o   *Serve the Gulai Kambing hot with steamed rice or your favorite bread.*

Sop Iga (Beef Ribs Soup)

Servings: 4 Time: 2-3 hours

Ingredients:

- *1 kg beef ribs, cut into pieces*
- *2 liters water*
- *2 carrots, peeled and sliced*
- *2 potatoes, peeled and cubed*
- *1 onion, chopped*
- *3 cloves garlic, minced*
- *2 tomatoes, chopped*
- *2 bay leaves*
- *Salt and pepper to taste*
- *Oil for cooking*
- *Fried shallots for garnish*
- *Chopped green onions for garnish*
- *Sliced red chilies (optional) for garnish*
- *Lime wedges for serving*

Directions:

1. *Prepare the Beef Ribs:*
   - *Rinse the beef ribs under cold water and pat them dry with paper towels.*

2. *Brown the Beef Ribs:*

   o *Heat oil in a large pot over medium-high heat. Add the beef ribs pieces and brown them on all sides. Remove and set aside.*

3. *Sauté Aromatics:*

   o *In the same pot, add a little more oil if needed. Sauté chopped onion and minced garlic until fragrant and translucent.*

4. *Cook the Soup:*

   o *Return the browned beef ribs to the pot. Add water, chopped tomatoes, bay leaves, sliced carrots, and cubed potatoes.*

   o *Bring the soup to a boil, then reduce heat to low. Cover and simmer for about 2-3 hours or until the beef ribs are tender and the vegetables are cooked through.*

5. *Season the Soup:*

   o *Season the Sop Iga with salt and pepper to taste. Adjust the seasoning according to your preference.*

6. *Serve:*

   o *Ladle the hot Sop Iga into serving bowls.*

   o *Garnish with fried shallots, chopped green onions, and sliced red chilies (if using).*

   o *Serve with lime wedges on the side for squeezing over the soup.*

DESSERTS

Es Teler (Mixed Fruit with Coconut and Avocado)

Servings: 4 Time: 30 minutes

Ingredients:

- *1 ripe avocado, peeled and cubed*
- *1 cup young coconut meat, cut into strips*
- *1 cup jackfruit, shredded*

- *1 cup sweetened condensed milk*
- *2 cups coconut milk*
- *Ice cubes*
- *Sugar (optional, to taste)*
- *Water (if needed to adjust consistency)*
- *Crushed ice (for serving)*

Directions:

1. *Prepare the Ingredients:*
   - *Peel and cube the ripe avocado.*
   - *Cut the young coconut meat into strips.*
   - *Shred the jackfruit.*
2. *Make the Coconut Milk Mixture:*
   - *In a bowl, mix together the coconut milk and sweetened condensed milk. Adjust sweetness with sugar if needed. Add water if the mixture is too thick.*
3. *Assemble the Es Teler:*
   - *In serving glasses or bowls, layer the avocado cubes, young coconut meat strips, and shredded jackfruit.*
   - *Pour the coconut milk mixture over the fruits until they are fully covered.*
4. *Add Ice:*
   - *Add ice cubes to the glasses or bowls to chill the dessert.*

5. *Serve:*

   o *Serve the Es Teler immediately with crushed ice on top for an extra refreshing touch.*

Klepon (Sweet Rice Balls with Palm Sugar)

Servings: Makes about 20-25 pieces Time: 1 hour

Ingredients:

- *1 cup glutinous rice flour*
- *1/4 cup rice flour (for coating)*
- *1 cup grated coconut (fresh or desiccated)*
- *150g palm sugar (gula jawa), cut into small cubes*
- *Pandan leaves or green food coloring (optional)*
- *Pinch of salt*
- *Water*

Directions:

1. *Prepare the Palm Sugar Filling:*
   - *In a bowl, combine the grated coconut with a pinch of salt. Mix well and set aside.*
   - *Take a small portion of palm sugar and wrap it in a ball shape with the grated coconut mixture. Repeat until all palm sugar is used. These will be the filling for the Klepon.*
2. *Make the Klepon Dough:*
   - *In a mixing bowl, combine the glutinous rice flour with a pinch of salt. Gradually add water and knead until*

you get a smooth and pliable dough. You may add pandan juice or green food coloring to the dough for color if desired.

3. **Form the Klepon:**

    o   *Take a small portion of the dough and flatten it in your palm.*

    o   *Place a palm sugar filling ball in the center of the dough and wrap the dough around it, forming a smooth ball. Ensure the palm sugar filling is completely covered by the dough.*

4. **Boil the Klepon:**

    o   *Bring a pot of water to a boil.*

    o   *Drop the Klepon balls into the boiling water. Cook until they float to the surface, about 2-3 minutes. Be careful not to overcrowd the pot; cook in batches if needed.*

5. **Coat the Klepon:**

    o   *Remove the cooked Klepon from the water and let them cool slightly.*

    o   *Roll the Klepon in rice flour to coat them evenly. This prevents them from sticking together and adds a nice texture.*

Dadar Gulung (Rolled Pandan Pancake with Sweet Coconut Filling)

Servings: Makes about 8-10 rolls Time: 45 minutes

Ingredients: For the Pancake Batter:

- *1 cup all-purpose flour*
- *1 cup coconut milk*
- *1/2 cup water*
- *2 tablespoons pandan juice (extracted from pandan leaves)*
- *2 tablespoons sugar*
- *1/4 teaspoon salt*
- *Green food coloring (optional)*

For the Sweet Coconut Filling:

- *2 cups grated coconut (fresh or desiccated)*
- *1/2 cup palm sugar (gula jawa), grated or chopped*
- *1/4 cup water*
- *Pandan leaves (optional, for flavor)*

For Cooking and Serving:

- *Butter or oil for cooking*
- *Additional grated coconut (for garnish, optional)*

Directions:

1. *Prepare the Sweet Coconut Filling:*
   - *In a saucepan, combine the grated coconut, palm sugar, water, and pandan leaves (if using). Cook over medium heat, stirring constantly, until the mixture is thick and the sugar has melted. Remove from heat and set aside to cool.*
2. *Make the Pancake Batter:*
   - *In a mixing bowl, whisk together the all-purpose flour, coconut milk, water, pandan juice, sugar, salt, and green food coloring (if using) until smooth. The batter should have a slightly thick consistency.*
3. *Cook the Pancakes:*
   - *Heat a non-stick skillet or frying pan over medium heat. Lightly grease the pan with butter or oil.*
   - *Pour a small ladleful of the pancake batter into the pan, swirling it around to form a thin, even layer. Cook for about 1-2 minutes until the edges start to lift and the surface appears set.*
   - *Carefully flip the pancake and cook for another 1-2 minutes until cooked through. Remove from the pan and repeat with the remaining batter.*
4. *Fill and Roll the Pancakes:*

- *Place a cooked pancake on a flat surface. Spoon a portion of the sweet coconut filling onto one end of the pancake.*
- *Roll the pancake tightly around the filling, folding in the sides as you roll to enclose the filling completely. Repeat with the remaining pancakes and filling.*

5. *Serve:*
   - *Slice the Dadar Gulung rolls into smaller pieces if desired.*
   - *Optionally, garnish with additional grated coconut on top.*

Lapis Legit (Layered Spice Cake)

Servings: Makes one 8-inch square cake Time: 3 hours

Ingredients:

- *400g unsalted butter, softened*
- *250g granulated sugar*
- *10 egg yolks*
- *150g all-purpose flour*
- *50g rice flour*
- *1 tablespoon condensed milk*
- *1 teaspoon vanilla extract*
- *1/2 teaspoon ground cinnamon*
- *1/4 teaspoon ground nutmeg*
- *1/4 teaspoon ground cloves*
- *1/4 teaspoon ground cardamom*
- *Pinch of salt*

Directions:

1. *Prepare the Pan:*
   - *Preheat your oven to 160°C (320°F). Grease and line an 8-inch square baking pan with parchment paper.*
2. *Cream the Butter and Sugar:*

o *In a large mixing bowl, cream together the softened butter and granulated sugar until light and fluffy.*

3. *Add Egg Yolks:*

   o *Add the egg yolks one at a time, mixing well after each addition until fully incorporated.*

4. *Add Dry Ingredients:*

   o *Sift the all-purpose flour, rice flour, ground cinnamon, ground nutmeg, ground cloves, ground cardamom, and a pinch of salt into the butter mixture. Fold gently until combined.*

5. *Add Flavorings:*

   o *Stir in the condensed milk and vanilla extract, mixing until the batter is smooth and well combined.*

6. *Layer the Batter:*

   o *Divide the batter into equal portions. You should have about 10-12 layers.*

   o *Spread a thin layer of batter evenly into the bottom of the prepared baking pan. Use a spatula to smooth it out.*

   o *Place the pan in the preheated oven and bake the first layer for about 5-7 minutes or until lightly golden and set.*

7. *Repeat Layering:*

- *Remove the pan from the oven and add another layer of batter on top of the baked layer. Spread it evenly and return the pan to the oven.*
- *Continue baking and layering until all the batter is used up, alternating between baking and adding layers until the cake is golden brown and cooked through. The top layer should be golden and slightly crispy.*

8. *Cool and Slice:*
   - *Once baked, remove the cake from the oven and let it cool completely in the pan.*
   - *Once cooled, carefully remove the cake from the pan and slice it into squares or rectangles to serve.*

Bubur Ketan Hitam (Black Sticky Rice Pudding)

Servings: 4-6 Time: 1 hour 30 minutes

Ingredients:

- *1 cup black glutinous rice (black sticky rice)*
- *4 cups water*
- *1 pandan leaf, tied into a knot (optional, for flavor)*
- *1/2 cup palm sugar (gula jawa), grated or chopped*
- *1/2 teaspoon salt*
- *1 cup coconut milk*
- *Toppings (optional):*
  - *Sliced ripe bananas*
  - *Toasted coconut flakes*
  - *Crushed peanuts or cashews*
  - *Additional palm sugar syrup*

Directions:

1. *Rinse and Soak the Black Glutinous Rice:*
   - *Rinse the black glutinous rice under cold water until the water runs clear.*
   - *Soak the rice in water for at least 4 hours or overnight. This helps soften the rice for cooking.*

2. *Cook the Black Sticky Rice:*

   o *In a large pot, bring 4 cups of water to a boil.*

   o *Add the soaked black glutinous rice and pandan leaf (if using) to the boiling water. Reduce heat to low and simmer, covered, for about 1 hour or until the rice is tender and cooked through. Stir occasionally to prevent sticking.*

3. *Sweeten the Rice:*

   o *Once the rice is cooked and softened, add grated or chopped palm sugar and salt to the pot. Stir well to combine and dissolve the sugar.*

   o *Continue simmering the rice for another 10-15 minutes until the palm sugar is fully incorporated and the rice pudding has a thick and creamy consistency.*

4. *Prepare the Coconut Milk:*

   o *In a separate saucepan, heat the coconut milk over low heat until warm. Do not boil.*

   o *You can sweeten the coconut milk with a little sugar if desired, or leave it unsweetened.*

5. *Serve:*

   o *Ladle the hot Bubur Ketan Hitam into serving bowls.*

   o *Drizzle the warm coconut milk over the rice pudding.*

   o *Optionally, top with sliced ripe bananas, toasted coconut flakes, crushed peanuts or cashews, and additional palm sugar syrup for extra sweetness and texture.*

Kue Lumpur (Mud Cake)

Servings: Makes about 12 cakes Time: 1 hour

Ingredients:

- *200g glutinous rice flour*
- *50g rice flour*
- *100g palm sugar (gula jawa), grated or chopped*
- *400ml coconut milk*
- *1/4 teaspoon salt*
- *Banana leaves or cupcake liners for lining*
- *Oil for greasing*

Directions:

1. *Prepare the Banana Leaves (if using):*
   - *If using banana leaves, cut them into square pieces slightly larger than your cupcake molds. Rinse and lightly steam or heat them to soften.*
2. *Make the Batter:*
   - *In a mixing bowl, combine the glutinous rice flour, rice flour, grated palm sugar, coconut milk, and salt. Mix well until smooth and no lumps remain.*
3. *Cook the Cake Batter:*

- o *Heat a non-stick pan or skillet over medium heat. Lightly grease the cupcake molds or line them with banana leaves or cupcake liners.*
- o *Pour the batter into the molds, filling each about 3/4 full.*

4. *Steam the Cakes:*

- o *Place the filled molds in a steamer basket or steaming rack.*
- o *Steam the Kue Lumpur over medium-high heat for about 20-25 minutes or until set and cooked through. Insert a toothpick into the center of a cake; if it comes out clean, the cakes are ready.*

5. *Cool and Serve:*

- o *Remove the Kue Lumpur from the steamer and let them cool slightly in the molds.*
- o *Once cooled, carefully remove the cakes from the molds or cupcake liners.*

Es Campur (Mixed Ice Dessert)

Servings: 4 Time: 15 minutes

Ingredients:

- *1 cup red agar-agar jelly (cut into cubes)*
- *1 cup green agar-agar jelly (cut into cubes)*
- *1 cup young coconut meat (cut into strips)*
- *1 cup jackfruit (shredded)*
- *1 cup sweetened condensed milk*
- *1 cup coconut milk*
- *Crushed ice*
- *Palm sugar syrup or simple syrup (optional, for extra sweetness)*
- *Other optional toppings:*
  - *Nata de coco (coconut jelly)*
  - *Grass jelly (cincau)*
  - *Sliced ripe bananas*
  - *Tapioca pearls (sago)*
  - *Diced avocado*

Directions:

1. *Prepare the Ingredients:*
   - *Cut the red and green agar-agar jelly into small cubes.*

- o *Cut the young coconut meat into strips.*
- o *Shred the jackfruit.*

2. *Mix the Ingredients:*
   - o *In a large mixing bowl, combine the red and green agar-agar jelly cubes, young coconut meat strips, shredded jackfruit, sweetened condensed milk, and coconut milk. Mix well to combine all the ingredients.*

3. *Assemble the Es Campur:*
   - o *In serving glasses or bowls, add a handful of crushed ice.*
   - o *Spoon the mixed ingredients (agar-agar jelly, coconut meat, jackfruit, and milk mixture) over the ice.*

4. *Add Toppings and Sweeteners:*
   - o *Optionally, drizzle palm sugar syrup or simple syrup over the Es Campur for extra sweetness.*
   - o *Add any additional toppings of your choice, such as nata de coco, grass jelly, sliced bananas, tapioca pearls, or diced avocado.*

5. *Serve:*
   - o *Serve the Es Campur immediately with a spoon or straw to enjoy the refreshing mix of flavors and textures.*

Martabak Telur (Stuffed Pancake)

Servings: Makes 1 large pancake (serves 2-4) Time: 45 minutes

Ingredients: For the Pancake Batter:

- *1 cup all-purpose flour*
- *1/2 teaspoon salt*
- *1 egg*
- *1 cup water*
- *Oil for cooking*

For the Filling:

- *200g ground beef or chicken*
- *1 small onion, finely chopped*
- *2 cloves garlic, minced*
- *1/2 teaspoon ground coriander*
- *1/2 teaspoon ground cumin*
- *1/2 teaspoon turmeric powder*
- *Salt and pepper to taste*
- *Oil for cooking*

For the Toppings (optional):

- *Sliced green onions*
- *Chopped cilantro*

- *Sambal or chili sauce*

Directions:

1. *Prepare the Pancake Batter:*
   - *In a mixing bowl, combine the all-purpose flour, salt, egg, and water. Whisk until smooth and no lumps remain. Set aside.*
2. *Make the Filling:*
   - *Heat a little oil in a pan over medium heat. Add the chopped onion and minced garlic. Sauté until fragrant and translucent.*
   - *Add the ground beef or chicken to the pan. Cook until browned and cooked through.*
   - *Stir in the ground coriander, ground cumin, turmeric powder, salt, and pepper. Mix well to combine all the spices with the meat. Cook for another minute. Remove from heat and set aside.*
3. *Cook the Pancake:*
   - *Heat a non-stick skillet or frying pan over medium heat. Add a little oil and swirl to coat the pan evenly.*
   - *Pour a ladleful of the pancake batter into the pan, spreading it out thinly to cover the bottom of the pan.*
4. *Add the Filling:*

- o *Spoon a generous amount of the cooked meat filling onto one half of the pancake in the pan. Spread it out evenly over the half.*

5. *Fold the Pancake:*
   - o *Carefully fold the other half of the pancake over the filling, creating a half-moon shape.*
   - o *Press down lightly with a spatula to seal the edges.*

6. *Cook Until Golden:*
   - o *Cook the Martabak Telur for a few minutes on each side until golden brown and crispy.*

7. *Serve:*
   - o *Transfer the cooked Martabak Telur to a cutting board. Slice into wedges or squares for serving.*
   - o *Optionally, garnish with sliced green onions, chopped cilantro, and serve with sambal or chili sauce on the side.*

Pisang Goreng (Fried Banana)

Servings: Makes about 4 servings Time: 20 minutes

Ingredients:

- *4 ripe bananas (choose firm bananas, such as plantains)*
- *1 cup all-purpose flour*
- *1/4 cup rice flour (for extra crispiness)*
- *1/4 cup cornstarch*
- *1/4 teaspoon salt*
- *1/2 teaspoon baking powder*
- *1 cup cold water (adjust as needed for batter consistency)*
- *Oil for frying*
- *Optional toppings:*
  - *Powdered sugar*
  - *Chocolate sauce*
  - *Cinnamon-sugar mixture*
- *Vanilla ice cream (for serving)*

Directions:

1. *Prepare the Bananas:*
   - *Peel the bananas and cut them into halves or thirds, depending on their size. You can also slice them lengthwise for longer pieces.*

2. *Make the Batter:*

   o *In a mixing bowl, combine the all-purpose flour, rice flour, cornstarch, salt, and baking powder.*

   o *Gradually add the cold water to the dry ingredients, whisking continuously until you get a smooth batter. The consistency should be thick enough to coat the banana slices.*

3. *Heat the Oil:*

   o *Heat enough oil in a deep frying pan or pot over medium-high heat. The oil should be hot but not smoking (around 350°F or 180°C).*

4. *Coat and Fry the Bananas:*

   o *Dip each banana slice into the batter, ensuring it is fully coated.*

   o *Carefully place the coated banana slices into the hot oil, one by one. Do not overcrowd the pan; fry in batches if needed.*

   o *Fry the bananas until golden brown and crispy, about 2-3 minutes per side. Use a slotted spoon to turn them halfway through cooking for even browning.*

5. *Drain and Serve:*

   o *Once fried to your desired crispness and golden color, remove the Pisang Goreng from the oil and drain them on a plate lined with paper towels to remove excess oil.*

o   *Serve the Fried Bananas hot as a snack or dessert.*

o   *Optionally, sprinkle with powdered sugar, drizzle with chocolate sauce or cinnamon-sugar mixture, or serve with a scoop of vanilla ice cream.*

Kolak Pisang (Banana in Coconut Milk)

Servings: Makes about 4 servings Time: 30 minutes

Ingredients:

- *4 ripe bananas, peeled and sliced*
- *400ml coconut milk*
- *200ml water*
- *100g palm sugar (gula jawa), grated or chopped*
- *1 pandan leaf, tied into a knot (optional, for flavor)*
- *Pinch of salt*
- *1/2 teaspoon vanilla extract*
- *1/4 teaspoon ground cinnamon (optional)*
- *Ice cubes (optional, for serving)*

Directions:

1. *Prepare the Ingredients:*
   - *Peel the bananas and slice them into rounds. Set aside.*
   - *In a saucepan, combine the coconut milk, water, grated palm sugar, pandan leaf (if using), pinch of salt, vanilla extract, and ground cinnamon (if using). Stir well to mix the ingredients.*
2. *Cook the Coconut Milk Mixture:*

- Place the saucepan over medium heat. Bring the coconut milk mixture to a gentle simmer, stirring occasionally to dissolve the palm sugar and infuse the flavors.

3. *Add the Bananas:*
   - Once the coconut milk mixture is simmering, add the sliced bananas to the saucepan.
   - Stir gently to coat the bananas with the coconut milk mixture.

4. *Simmer Until Bananas Are Tender:*
   - Allow the bananas to simmer in the coconut milk mixture for about 5-7 minutes or until they are tender but not mushy. Stir occasionally to prevent sticking.

5. *Check Sweetness and Adjust:*
   - Taste the Kolak Pisang and adjust the sweetness if needed by adding more palm sugar according to your preference.

6. *Serve:*
   - Once the bananas are tender and the flavors have melded, remove the pandan leaf (if used) from the saucepan.
   - Optionally, transfer the Kolak Pisang to a serving bowl and let it cool slightly.
   - Serve the Kolak Pisang warm or chilled. You can also add ice cubes to the serving bowl for a refreshing twist.

MEASURES

1. **Volume Conversions:**
   - *1 cup = 240 milliliters*
   - *1 tablespoon = 15 milliliters*
   - *1 teaspoon = 5 milliliters*
   - *1 fluid ounce = 30 milliliters*

2. **Weight Conversions:**
   - *1 ounce = 28 grams*
   - *1 pound = 453 grams*
   - *1 kilogram = 2.2 pounds*

3. **Temperature Conversions:**

- *Celsius to Fahrenheit: F = (C × 9/5) + 32*

- *Fahrenheit to Celsius: C = (F − 32) × 5/9*

4. **Length Conversions:**

- *1 inch = 2.54 centimeters*

- *1 foot = 30.48 centimeters*

- *1 meter = 39.37 inches*

5. **Common Ingredient Conversions:**

- *1 stick of butter = 1/2 cup = 113 grams*

- *1 cup of flour = 120 grams*

- *1 cup of sugar = 200 grams*

6. **Oven Temperature Conversions:**

- *Gas Mark 1 = 275°F = 140°C*

- *Gas Mark 2 = 300°F = 150°C*

- *Gas Mark 4 = 350°F = 180°C*

- *Gas Mark 6 = 400°F = 200°C*

- *Gas Mark 8 = 450°F = 230°C*

Made in the USA
Las Vegas, NV
05 December 2024

13304482R00079